KEEPING TOM NICE

KEEPING TOM NICE

by Lucy Gannon

JOSEF WEINBERGER PLAYS

LONDON

KEEPING TOM NICE
First published in 1990
by Josef Weinberger Ltd
(pka Warner/Chappell Plays Ltd)
12-14 Mortimer Street, London, W1T 3JJ
www.josef-weinberger.com
general.info@jwmail.co.uk

ISBN 978-0-85676-146-1

For Gerald and Norah Gannon
And
In Memory Of
Mary Gannon

KEEPING TOM NICE was first presented by the Royal
Shakespeare Company at the Almeida Theatre, London on
9th August, 1988, with the following cast:

TOM	Linus Roache
CHARLIE	Henrietta Bess
WINNIE	Shirley King
DOUG	Richard Conway
STEPHEN	Mike Dowling

Directed by Bill Buffrey
Designed by Louise Belson
Lighting by Geraint Pughe

*   *   *   *   *   *

The play takes place in an acting area, rather than a set.
Only what is required is present. The time is free flowing,
telescopic.

In the first half of the play, until Stephen enters the house,
we can see him around the action – not a part of it, but
there.

AUTHORS NOTE

People have grown used to thinking about and 'caring about' people who have genius, apparently, but are trapped within a disabled, wayward or non-functioning body. Tom isn't one of these geniuses. He's you or me, the person who serves us in the market or the man who sweeps the street, he could be within the accepted norms of intelligence or he could perhaps struggle to understand the simplest of sums. He has the right to be mentally ordinary or even dull just as he has the right to be an intellectual giant, and his dilemma is no less whichever he is. I do not believe that a person with high intelligence is any more precious or deserving of our care and understanding and compassion than someone with learning difficulties or an impaired understanding of the world. We're all in the soup together bright and dull alike, none of us have earned the brains we've got, so why all the desire to see something 'extra-ordinary' in people like Tom, as if it is only this which deserves our attention? Few of us would ever get a glance from the rest of the world if this was true.

Having said that, the play is not about Tom. It is about looking after Tom, what that does to him and his family.

Lucy Gannon
April, 1990.

THE DISCORDS

An infra red camera can take a night photograph of a car
park after a hot day and show where cars have been
parked, reproducing an impression of them. The discords
are what remain in the house after 24 years of this family
living in it, doing the same things at the same times of day,
saying the same words, the same pattern of words, thinking
the same things, dreaming private dreams, for all that time.
They are not happening in Tom's head, or anyone else's,
some of the words have actually been said, some of them
have remained unspoken, some they have not dared to say,
but they are all real. I call them discords because the
characters appear to be talking, to be answering each other,
but in fact each phrase just skids off the next, each person
deflects the words of the others with heart-breaking,
unthinking skill. The unreality of these discords become
apparent in the words, and shouldn't be self-consciously
presented, as if their meaning is portentous, or more
important than the rest of the play. The discords are the
flotsam of four lives, that's all – they're not consciously
presented to the world, and they are therefore revealing.

CHARACTERS

DOUG–Tom's father. Aged about 60. A well educated man, middle class, used to be a middle manager in an engineering business and took early retirement to help look after Tom.

TOM–A man of 24. Severely physically disabled, unable to communicate, to feed or tend to himself, to walk or pick anything up even. We don't know how intelligent Tom is, but we know he uses language internally.

WINNIE–Tom's mother. Aged about 55. A pleasant, capable woman who has not had a career other than looking after Tom and the rest of her family.

CHARLIE–Tom's sister. 23 years old. Living away from home at university. She went to university late after working in an office for a couple of years and caught up with her A level exams at evening school. Doug always believed that she would go to university and it was to please him, to 'make up' for Tom that she persevered and finally got there. A bright, apparently loving but immature woman.

STEPHEN–Tom's social worker.

Photograph by Ivan Kyncl from the RSC production of KEEPING TOM NICE

SCENE ONE

First Discord (TOM'S)

TOM, *alone, in his wheelchair. Dark, growing gradually lighter but still dim until* DOUG *draws the curtains.*

TOM Tom's here. Tom's here. Here. Juddering Tom. Dancing Tom. Jerking, juddering Tom, here. Tom sore bones. Bones. Bones aching in secret places. Bones boning in boney places. Razor bones on paper skin. Tom. Tom's here. Here. Daybreak Tom. Moonlight Tom. Just Tom.

(*We hear a noise in the distance.* TOM *is quiet for a moment.*)

Daddy! Daddy! Dark. Dark as Daddy. Dark. Dark. Father. (*Exploring the word.*) Father. Father? Fa..the..er. Dad. Daddy. Daddy father. Daddy! How many thoughts to morning? Sore bones, sore skin, sore, sore. Juddering-jerking, splaying, twisting, sore. Cold, dry, empty sore. Dry. Tom dry, dying for a cold wet gasping grabbing gulp. Tom. Poor Tom. Tom's cup. My cup. Sing-a-song, Tom, my cup. See Stephen-here-to-help-you, Tom's cup.

CHARLIE (*off, coming on, stepping out from the shadows*) Look, He's reaching for his cup.

(TOM *looks around, straining his neck, his eyes rolling backwards his head lolls back and he strains to reach the cup, his movements tiny but ladened with effort.*)

CHARLIE He's stretching for his cup.

WINNIE (*off, coming on, stepping out from the shadows*) No good telling me dear, I can't hear you. Can't hear you.

CHARLIE Look! Look!

WINNIE I can't hear you dear, no good telling me.

CHARLIE	Tom! Yay! Tom!
	(TOM *laughs on the intake of a breath.*)
WINNIE	It's no good, dear, he can't hear you. Can't hear you.
CHARLIE	Stretching, straining, looking.
WINNIE	Jerking.
CHARLIE	Trying.
WINNIE	I meant to change his jumper.
CHARLIE	He's trying to pick up his bloody cup!
TOM	Tom's cup Charlie! (*He jerks back in frustration, a wordless yell.*)
WINNIE	I like him to look nice.
DOUG	(*off, coming on*) He looks nice.
CHARLIE	Don't you see? Don't you see?
DOUG	He looks alright. He is alright!
CHARLIE	He's reaching for his cup, are you blind?
WINNIE	I can't hear you, dear. I can't see. I choose not to listen, dear. I like to keep him nice.
	(TOM, *exhausted, allows his fingers to droop. Suddenly, cruelly, full light floods in, as* DOUG *wrenches back the curtains.* TOM *screws up his eyes in protest, his fingers splay again.*)
DOUG	We do keep him nice. (*He goes to* TOM *and smiles down at him. His fingers play with* TOM'S, *tip to tip. He leans over and rubs* TOM'S *stubble playfully.*) Pushing the razor firmly over....and up....under the chin....pull his nose to get that bit there....
	(TOM *snorts with laughter.*)
WINNIE	That bit there.
DOUG	I know. On the humps of his jaw bones, little circles.

WINNIE	Oh, yes, he does look nice.
DOUG	(*admiring* TOM'S *jumper*) Good colour that.
WINNIE	Royal blue.
DOUG	Uniform blue. Smart and clean. (*He briskly mimes putting a jumper on* TOM, *practised in the task, crisp and efficient.*) Take his hand and push the sleeve on. . . . so. Take the neck, hold it open, ease it over his head. Lolling, sad head. The other hand. . . . so. Pull it all down. . .
WINNIE	There! That's it! Smart as a pin.
DOUG	(*smiling into* TOM'S *face*) Clean as a whistle.
WINNIE	Bright as a button.
CHARLIE	Mad as a hatter. Daft as a brush. Silent as the grave.
	(*She looks at* TOM *and pulls a face. He shouts, a sudden happy shout.*)
WINNIE	We like to keep him nice. We'll always keep him nice.
DOUG	For ever and ever.
CHARLIE	Amen.
	(*They look at* TOM *and he looks back, anxious. His fingers and his head move in concern. They move nearer, peering at him. He closes his eyes.*)

SCENE TWO

TOM'S *Room. While this scene is going on* WINNIE *bustles around the room tidying up, getting rid of the talcum, the brush, flannel etc.* DOUG *watches her, a bone china tea cup and saucer in his hand. He is absentmindedly dunking a biscuit.*

WINNIE	I wish you wouldn't wander around with that cup in your hands, Doug.

DOUG	What do you want me to do with it? I tried balancing it on my head, but I can't see where I'm dunking my biscuits.
WINNIE	And that's a disgusting habit, anyway.
DOUG	I know. It gives you crumbs down your parting. Shall I give Tom a drink before I go?
WINNIE	It's too hot.
DOUG	I'm in no hurry.
WINNIE	I'll do it.
DOUG	Don't forget.
WINNIE	I don't forget. I never forget. What do you mean? (*She goes to a low table and moves a vase of flowers so that they are exactly central.*)
DOUG	Nothing. Another of those bloody pamphlets this morning. Wasting rate payer's money.
WINNIE	What was it this time?
DOUG	Some damn thing. (*He sees that she isn't watching and moves the flowers a couple of inches so that* TOM *can see them from his chair.*) Holidays or days out or social evenings. I don't know. Didn't read it. They're all the same.
WINNIE	You'd think that they'd have realised by now. There must be people who need them, people who'd be glad of being remembered. People who *need* them.
DOUG	We're on the list, see. Once you're on the list. . . remember how The Reader's Digest was calling my dad a most valued customer when he'd been dead twelve years? They get your name and that's it.
WINNIE	Oh, yes, *them*. But you'd think that social services had more sense.

DOUG	Charities. Half the time it's charities. There's a charity for everything these days. And self-help groups.
WINNIE	(*going to* TOM, *as if to lift up the rug around his legs*) Did you do his bag?
DOUG	I'll do it. My job. Leave it alone.
WINNIE	(*she lifts the rug anyway and then drops it back down*) There's hardly anything in it.
DOUG	I know. Self-help groups and discussion groups, support groups, associations. You can't get a boil on your bum without half a dozen committees standing around you, looking at it, and giving out information sheets.
WINNIE	(*stopping and enjoying the joke*) And people knocking on the door, wanting to tell you how big their boils are!
DOUG	'Giving mutual support' they call it.
WINNIE	Crying on each other's shoulders, more like.
DOUG	That's how minorities are born, Winnie. 'Civil rights for bum boils!' 'Positive discrimination for bum boils!'
WINNIE	'Holidays by the sea for bum boils!'
	(*They are silent for a split second.*)
DOUG	Ah, yes, holidays.
WINNIE	(*bustling on*) I wish they'd leave us alone, I do. We're alright aren't we? What does Tom want with a holiday?
DOUG	Nothing. I'd better be off. Meals on wheels don't wait, and you know what the oldies are like if the stuff isn't actually on the boil.
WINNIE	Go carefully then.
DOUG	Always. (*He goes to* TOM *and looks at him fondly.*)

WINNIE   And wear your jacket.

DOUG   Be a good boy for Mum, eh? (*He gives* TOM's
              cheek a little pat. It's too sharp and TOM *jerks.*
              DOUG *touches him, gentler.*)

WINNIE   (*watching this small exchange but then turning
              away*) I'll get his drink.

              (DOUG *and* WINNIE *exit.* WINNIE *returns almost
              immediately with the drink in a baby cup. She sits
              to the side of him, shakes out a pink bib, puts it
              around his neck. Notices the flowers and moves
              them back so that they are central again but out of*
              TOM's *vision. She smiles into his face.*)

WINNIE   There! That's better, isn't it? Now. A nice
              cup of tea.

                          SCENE THREE

STEPHEN *is working a stencilling machine, watching the copies as
they come off, the strenuous movement of turning the handle
mirroring his thoughts. We can hear the buzz of conversation,
typewriters, laughter and phones ringing in the distance.*

STEPHEN   I find myself thinking about him all the time.
              In a meeting about someone else, some other
              problem, thinking about him. I look at
              strangers in the street, and I think of Tom. I
              go to a case meeting for someone entirely
              different. Different person. Different needs.
              Different . . . . and my thoughts are all on
              Tom. Wondering what he's doing. What
              they're doing. They always put his chair in
              the same place. Facing the same way, seeing
              the same things, looking at the same patch of
              carpet. The same strip of wallpaper.
              Whenever I visit, there he is. I turned his
              chair around once, and showed him the open
              window, the curtains fluttering in the
              summer breeze, but she came back in, his
              mother, and with a deft flick of the wrist she
              had him back to where he always sits. A
              quick flick. Like that.

WINNIE	(*sitting by* TOM, *still, smiling over at* STEPHEN) The sun. The sun hurts his eyes.
STEPHEN	'The garden,' I said, 'so that he can see the garden.'
WINNIE	'Goodness Stephen!'
STEPHEN	In that bright, cheerful, patent leather, Marks and Spencers voice, 'He can't see everything'. Picking up his foot, which had dared to slip sideways, and slamming it down on the metal rest. (*Slam.*)
WINNIE	Goodness me, dear. There's bound to be something he can't see. (*She exits.*)
STEPHEN	Only the world. Only the whole damn world.

SCENE FOUR

Tom's *Room.* TOM *is dozing in his chair. Room pristine as before. We hear the front door open and* DOUG *enters the room, goes to stand over* TOM *who is awake now, grinning at him, mild spasm.*

DOUG	(*calling*) I'm back! (*He touches* TOM's *hand and then takes off his outdoor clothes.*)
WINNIE	(*off*) I'm just mincing Tom's dinner.
DOUG	(*hanging his clothes up in the hall*) Any visitors? (*He comes back into the room and calls again.*) Any visitors?
WINNIE	(*entering*) Of course not.
DOUG	I thought that Stephen bloke might call today.
WINNIE	(*putting a bib on* TOM) No.
DOUG	He was a nice enough young man. (*Takes the dinner, to* WINNIE's *mild annoyance, pulls a chair up and sits down to feed* TOM.) 'Course , they all are. Nice and young.
WINNIE	(*mischief making*) I had the feeling that he was criticising.

DOUG	Criticising?
WINNIE	Looking. And thinking. You know. And when he went he said he hoped he'd see a lot of us.
DOUG	They've all said that, love. I'll believe it when I see it. There was that bloke, oh, a couple of years back .... we were going to see him every day, remember?
WINNIE	Oh, yes, that psychologist. What was his name?
DOUG	He was going to work bloody miracles. Come here every day, assess this, assess that, measure every damn thing. How often did we see him?
WINNIE	I think he got disheartened: that great pile of forms to fill in, thousands of little ticks–
DOUG	In thousands of little boxes!
WINNIE	And Tom couldn't do anything. Tom couldn't do a single thing. (*To her this is a simple statement, to* DOUG *it is a cause of terrible sadness which, his back to her, she doesn't see.*) I think he lost heart.
DOUG	They all lose heart, love. Same as this one will, this Stephen.
WINNIE	(*indignant*) He said he couldn't see the garden.
DOUG	Stephen did?
WINNIE	I came in and he'd moved Tom's chair.
DOUG	(*pulling a small face at* TOM) Well, never mind.
WINNIE	And his eyes. They look him up and down. Stephen looks up and down Tom and seems to take everything in. You can see him thinking.

DOUG	(*more interested, less patronising*) What do you mean?
WINNIE	I came in from the kitchen and that Stephen was holding Tom's hand, sort of rubbing it with his thumb, and then he pushed the sleeve up and looked at his wrist.
DOUG	(*stopping abruptly*) He's had enough. What did he say?
WINNIE	(*looking at the food remaining*) Who?
DOUG	Stephen! What did he say?
WINNIE	When?
DOUG	When he was stroking Tom's hand – what did he say?
WINNIE	(*turning to go, taking the food dish*) Nothing. He didn't say anything. I'll put our lunch in the sitting room.
DOUG	I'll be right there. Tom's just about ready for a little nap. Aren't you Tom?

(*He's taking* TOM'S *bib off wiping* TOM'S *mouth with a damp flannel, with restrained violence.*) Aren't you, Tom? Ready for a 'little nap'. (*Struggling to keep his temper.*) These bloody social workers. What do you make of them, Tom? Do you like them, Tom? These bloody social workers?

(*Slamming about now, pushing* TOM'S *footrests up, putting* TOM'S *feet on a stool, placing a cushion under them, all caring tasks performed angrily.*)

At the end of the day, though, where are they? At meal times where are they? These precious bloody experts, eh? Where's precious bloody Stephen now? Now, when you need feeding. Now, when you need changing? God! (*Face thrust into* TOM'S.) You stink! I said where is he now? Now that

you're stinking? Bloody stinking? Don't look
at me! Don't you look at me! (*Takes* TOM's
head and pushes it to one side so that TOM's
looking at the wall.) Don't you fucking look at
me!

(*Aghast at his own behaviour but unable to stop,*
DOUG *strides to the back of the chair, trying to
leave* TOM *alone. Unable to, he shoves his face up
against* TOM's *again.*) Useless! Useless!
Senseless, fucking useless!

(*During the last three words* WINNIE *has come to
the doorway.*)

WINNIE   (*brightly, smoothly*) Come on, you boys. Our
sandwiches are curling up and dying. And I
thought Tom was going to have a nap?
(*Drawing the curtains.*) I don't know, I really
don't.

DOUG   (*going*) I'll wash my hands.

WINNIE   Well, don't be long. (*She takes a long look at*
TOM *on the way out.*)

(TOM *sits alone, crying.*)

SCENE FIVE

STEPHEN *is standing, looking at* TOM *in the distance.*

STEPHEN   The first time I saw him, with his hair about
his face, like sea weed on a drowned man,
and his John The Baptist eyes, he caught me.
Caught me with the eyes and the face of a
prophet. They were getting him out of the
bath, his long thin body, Christ's body, taken
down from the cross and washed for burial.
His Mother, like Mary Magdalen, no idea
who the hell he was, saint or sinner, Messiah
or man. And his father, shirt sleeves rolled
up, red faced and sweating in the steam.
Nightmare. Just another client. Nightmare.

SCENE SIX

First Discord ending. All are standing at a distance from TOM.

CHARLIE   Mad as a hatter. Daft as a brush. Silent as the
            grave.

WINNIE   We like to keep him nice. We'll always keep
            him nice.

DOUG   For ever and ever.

CHARLIE   Amen.

WINNIE   He's not in bed! (*She goes up to* TOM.) He's
            not in bed and the news half done. The
            weather soon.

DOUG   After the news.

WINNIE   But he's not in bed!

DOUG   Just for tonight. He's alright. Just for tonight.
            (WINNIE *takes hold of* TOM'S *legs, waits for*
            DOUG *to take his body. Unwillingly, he does. They*
            lift him onto the bed.)

CHARLIE   Oh, listen to me. He's trying to reach.

WINNIE   Not a good idea, Doug.

CHARLIE   He's doing.

WINNIE   Bed sores.

DOUG   Just for tonight, no soap and flannel and one
            two three . . .

TOM   Sore bones.

            (*They stop for an instant, then carry on.*)

DOUG   Just for tonight?

WINNIE   First time ever. Thin end of the wedge. Thin
            end of the slippery slope, I say.

DOUG   After twenty four years – a breather.

STEPHEN	I thought they'd jump at the chance. A week away from it all. Not much, but still, a breather. I thought they'd grab at it, but she said.
WINNIE	We'd worry about him so much.
STEPHEN	And he gave his tight little smile–
DOUG	Thanks all the same.
STEPHEN	And my words hang in the air between us all, "Well, if you change your minds ... have second thoughts", and she smooths an imagined crease in the curtains.
STEPHEN WINNIE	} (*together*) "Oh, no, we'd miss Tom."
	(*Pause.*)
STEPHEN	(*small shrug*) Helpless.

SCENE SEVEN

TOM'S *Room. Daytime. We hear the front door open, slam back on its hinges.*

CHARLIE	(*Off*) Yoo hoo! It's me! (TOM *crows with delight, slight spasm. We hear a bag being dumped.*)
DOUG	Charlotte? Winnie it's Charlotte!
CHARLIE	Hang on ...(CHARLIE *enters like a whirlwind. Runs straight to the bed.*)
	Tom! Tom! Oh Tommy Tom. Here I am!
	(TOM *is screaming with laughter now. She takes his hands and kisses his face, gives him a little shake, laughing back.*)
	Hello, you bugger. Here I am. Sort you out! Sort you out once and for all. Shake you up. (*He screams again. She hugs him.*) Oh, it's good to see you. (*Singing and playing with* TOM.) It is good to see you. Missed me? Missed me? Shall I sing? Shall I? (*Sings.*) "Oh, soldier,

soldier, will you marry me, With your musket
fife and drum?" "Oh, no, sweet maid, I canna
marry you, For I have no clothes to put on."
So, off she went, to her Grandfather's chest,
And she brought him some clothes of the
very very best And the soldier put them on.
OOOOOh, soldier, soldier ... will you marry
me? (*She turns it into a mix-type song, repeating
it, jumping up and 'moon walking'.*) Will you.
Will you. Will you. Oh, soldier. Soldier.
Marry me? Marry me? Marry me? (*He is
laughing and now she joins in, falling down to
rock him in time to her song.*) With your musket
fife and drum? Oh, no, sweet maid, I cannot
marry you, for I have a wife of my own.
There. That was a lullaby. Darling Tom. As
handsome as ever. Have you missed me? I
bet you have. I bet, if you could manage it,
you'd give me such a hug and you'd say,
'Charlotte! God, I have missed you!'
Wouldn't you?

STEPHEN   I want to get him away from there.

CHARLIE   Oh, I want to get you away.

STEPHEN   Out into the world.

CHARLIE   Wheel you along the road.

STEPHEN   Let him feel the rain on his cheeks.

CHARLIE   Take you to a disco.

STEPHEN   Lie him on the beach.

CHARLIE   So you can smell the sweat and the stale beer.

STEPHEN   So that he feels the wind in his hair and the
salt on his lips. I do.

CHARLIE   I do. (*She hugs Tom again.*)

STEPHEN   But it's easier to lie awake at night worrying
about that tight little home than it is to visit
it. I sense something. And it stops me. It
stops me in mid breath. I can't go in and

snatch him out. And I can't stand by and mutely observe. And I can't get him out of my mind.

(DOUG *enters with* TOM's *meal on a tray.*)

DOUG   Off the bed, Charlotte. I wish you wouldn't do that.

CHARLIE   Me? Do what, Dad?

DOUG   You know full well what. We've told you often enough. Mauling him.

CHARLIE   Mauling him? Is that what I was doing? I was just saying hello, after being away for weeks and weeks.

DOUG   Sisters don't greet their brothers like that.

CHARLIE   Oh, God.

DOUG   It's not healthy.

CHARLIE   Bearing in mind that he's totally immobile, spastic, epileptic, and incontinent – oh, and aphasic – that's bloody funny, Dad. Really pertinent, that is.

DOUG   You know what I mean.

CHARLIE   Yes. I know what you mean. I'll go and unpack.

DOUG   How does he look, Tom?

CHARLIE   Frail. Frailer than I'd remembered.

DOUG   He's been poorly. He chokes a lot now, and he's losing weight. At night he shouts. Suddenly yells.

CHARLIE   Why?

DOUG   Who knows? With Tom, who knows? I think he's weary of it all.

CHARLIE   And you, Dad, are you weary of it all?

DOUG   What?

CHARLIE	What do you think of retirement?
DOUG	I don't think of it, love. I just live it. It's not so bad. I've got my greenhouse.
CHARLIE	And what about all your plans? The holidays in Scotland, the evenings out, the chess club? You were going to be so busy.
DOUG	We can't leave Tom. I thought that we could, but, when it comes down to it – we can't.
CHARLIE	Dad, the social services said that they'd take care of him, didn't they? Just an evening or two a week.
DOUG	I can't hand him over to a 'they'. I thought you were going to unpack? (CHARLIE *starts to go out but hesitates.*)
CHARLIE	Are you undressing him?
DOUG	We always undress him. You know that. Would you like to go to bed in all your clothes?
CHARLIE	I just thought. You always had him ready for bed so early.
DOUG	Yes, well, I always went to bed so early too, didn't I? So I could get up again at five o'clock to get Tom washed and dressed and in his chair before I left for work at seven o'clock. But I don't have to do that any more, do I? So now I sit with your Mother and watch TV for a while, OK? And after tea I lie him on his bed so that he gets a rest from that damn chair. And at supper time we heave him onto his bean bag so that he gets another little change. OK? Is that alright?
CHARLIE	Dad! Don't be so bloody touchy! I mean, I'm glad he stays up a bit longer ... I only wondered, that's all – and I get a bloody lecture! (*She stomps off.*)

DOUG   When she was born, Tom, your sister, you
              were thirteen months old. We'd just been
              told about you, your Mother and me. Well,
              told as much as they knew, which wasn't
              much. Your Mother couldn't stop crying. She
              held Charlotte in her arms and cried for you.
              And I was angry. So bloody angry. We
              couldn't welcome her for grieving for you,
              and we couldn't grieve for you for welcoming
              her. Guilty on all bloody counts. I took you
              in to see her on the day that she was born.
              You weren't much bigger than her. It gave us
              a shock to see that. We laid you side by side
              on the bed. Introduced you. Same hair. Same
              features. Same perfect little hands. And I
              thought my heart would break. I thought my
              heart would break, Tom. Like a sword had
              been plunged through me. Agony. Agony so
              bad I wanted to scream and cry out and
              clutch myself together, clutch myself
              together. Scream and cry and shit. It clawed
              at my stomach and twisted my bowels, so that
              I wanted to shit. Grabbed my bowels,
              wrenched the heart from me, wrung me out.
              There's no pain like that, Tom, not in this
              world. To look at the two of you, lying there,
              there's no grief like that. It's not to be
              endured. Even now, it's not to be endured,
              even now. And it doesn't go away. Ever. Like
              a sword had been plunged through me. "And
              a sword will pierce your own heart, too."
              That's the bloody word you sent to your
              handmaiden. That's the message you sent to
              Mary. A sword to pierce her heart. And
              mine! God! At least she saw her son 'grow in
              stature'. She saw him walk, she saw him run,
              she heard him talk. Words from his lips. I'd
              let them crucify you for that, Tom. Oh, God,
              I'd let them crucify you for that. I'd drive the
              nails in for that! For one bloody word. Here!
              Give me the hammer, the nails, the cross!
              Give them to me! I'll do it! I'll bloody do it!

For just one word, I'll crucify my Tom. I
offer him to you. For just one word. I offer
him. My son. My son. My beloved son. My
beloved son. (*He rests exhausted.* TOM *smiles
uncertainly.*)

SCENE EIGHT

DOUG *slowly recovers and feeds* TOM *his meal, spooning in the
food with great patience, his back to* CHARLIE *who has entered and
is slouched in* TOM'S *wheelchair, rocking it. She puts her foot up
on a piece of furniture, watching* DOUG *critically. Now and then*
DOUG *gives* TOM *a small smile, a moue.*

CHARLIE	Why don't you ever talk to him?
DOUG	What sort of a question is that?
CHARLIE	A simple one. You never talk to him.
DOUG	If you say so.
CHARLIE	Oh, God!
DOUG	If you say so, it must be true mustn't it? Who could deny the truth of your words? Fresh from Olympus. (*Seeing her foot.*) Foot down.
CHARLIE	(*automatically obeying*) If he was a dog you'd talk to him.
DOUG	(*tidying the tray, the meal finished*) If he was a dog he'd feed himself. If he was a dog he'd go for walks. If he was a dog he'd bring me the bloody paper. As it is . . . it doesn't matter.
CHARLIE	It does matter. It matters that you think less of my brother than you would of a dog–
DOUG	I didn't say that.
CHARLIE	I heard that.
DOUG	I can't help what you heard. (*He starts to lift the rug on* TOM'S *leg but then stops.*) If you could just pop out for a moment?

CHARLIE   Oh, God, here we go. The ritual of the bag.
             For God's sake, Dad, it's not incestuous for
             me to see my brother's piss.

DOUG   Charlotte!

CHARLIE   Sor-ry. Ur-ine. But we both know you're
             going to empty his bag. I've done it
             thousands of times. Me and Mum.

DOUG   Thank you. Thank you for that reminder,
             Charlotte. That 'In case you've forgotten, you
             senile old fool'. Do you think that I don't
             know? Do you think that I don't know how
             often you and your Mother have tipped away
             his urine? I courted her once, to the sounds
             of Glenn Miller. I promised her the earth, to
             love and to cherish, to hold and to protect
             and to love, to the sounds of Glenn Miller.
             Do you really think that I don't know how
             many times she's tipped away my son's urine?
             Alright! here it is! (*He lifts the rug, and
             brandishes the catheter bag.*) A bag full of piss,
             as you bright, bloody young things would say.
             The total achievement of Tom's young life.
             The end result of every day and night, every
             day and night for the last twenty four years.
             Not much, some would say, but you can't
             fault his consistency. Can't do a lot, our Tom,
             but by God you should see him pee! We
             could get up coach parties! Fantastic peeing
             record holder! Pees all day long in the
             privacy of his own room! Steadily, stealthily,
             while you all think he's wasting his time, he's
             secretly peeing! Mind you, he's not the man
             he was. Time was, he didn't have a piss bag.
             Time was, you'd go into him at ten-to-six in
             the morning, and you'd find the bed all nice
             and warm and dry and you'd offer up a silent
             prayer, and creep over for the bottle, and
             creep back again, and try to carefully, ever so
             carefully, ease the bottle in, ease him into the
             bottle, and then ... just as it was

nearly ... ever so nearly ... there, he'd open
his eyes, look straight at you, and let out a
bloody bucketful. All over the place. Bloody
gallons. But now, of course, he has a bag.
And on dull days, when you're away at
university, learning how bloody stupid the
rest of us are, we sit around in here watching
him pee.

(*Pause.*)

CHARLIE   I'm sorry.

DOUG   I talk to him. Sometimes. After twenty four
years there's not a hell of a lot I haven't
already told him. There's not a hell of a lot I
can do for him, either, but at least I can give
him some degree of dignity, privacy. At least
I can do that much. Oh, I can't give him the
sort of love you give him. I can't discount the
years, the deadly routine, the tons of mush
I've spooned into him, the tons of muck I've
coaxed out, the rivers of urine I've tipped
away. I can't discount it. All the weight and
warmth and stink of it for all his life.

So be a good girl and humour your old Dad,
would you? Bugger off while I empty this
bloody bag. (CHARLIE *goes slowly, thoughtfully,
while* DOUG *empties the bag into a plastic jug.*
TOM *gurgles at him.*)

DOUG   (*smiling at* TOM) 'Pisssssssssssss.'

(*At the end of the hiss he pulls a face at* TOM.
TOM *laughs but almost immediately his eyelids
droop.* DOUG *looks at him for a moment, stoney
faced.*)

SCENE NINE

Second Discord (CHARLIE'S)

Everything DOUG *and* WINNIE *say here is a cliche, a phrase*
TOM's *heard perhaps a hundred times. Everything* CHARLIE *says
has been whispered to him alone. And so* DOUG *and* WINNIE

speak out while CHARLIE *tends to speak quietly, just to* TOM *until* DOUG *and* WINNIE *are drawn into it.*

CHARLIE	At night I dream of him. In the day I think of him. Little things remind me.
WINNIE	That's nice.
CHARLIE	Little things. The smell of a soap. The curve of a man's chin. Hairs on an arm.
WINNIE	It's nice to think of him.
CHARLIE	The man smell of a young man.
DOUG	I choose not to hear that.
CHARLIE	The man smell of a young man. I choose to say it.
WINNIE	Goodness.
CHARLIE	Harmless things. The smell of soap.
TOM	Charlie. (*They don't hear.*)
CHARLIE	And I can't stop the thoughts.
DOUG	Charlotte!
WINNIE	Least said soonest mended.
DOUG	Best left unsaid.
WINNIE	Such a pretty name, Charlotte.
TOM	Charlie. Charlie chatterbox. (*They don't hear.*)
CHARLIE	The curve of a man's chin, hairs on an arm, the smell of a man, the smell of his soap, the tang of his sweat.
DOUG	Charlie.
CHARLIE	Reminders. The feel of him. The flesh of him.
WINNIE	We chose that name because it was so sweet. Charlotte.
CHARLIE	And the man who fills me, prods me, sweats on me, the man who holds me, breathes beer

on me, pierces me, lies on me too long and whose skin melts onto mine in cold and sweaty union, becomes Tom.

DOUG You know I don't like you doing that.

CHARLIE When he's lain on me too long, and the pleasure has been shot, and our bodies are replete with the sameness of it all, I feel as if I have no strength, no breath, and as if the body crushing mine is Tom. (DOUG *has been combing* TOM'S *hair and lets* TOM'S *head fall back*.)

DOUG You know I don't like you doing that.

CHARLIE (*close*) As if it is Tom who saps all my strength.

WINNIE A nasty dream.

TOM My dream.

CHARLIE A harmless dream.

DOUG Off the bed, Charlotte.

TOM Into bed, Charlotte.

WINNIE I thought we'd have such fun.

CHARLIE I only want to comfort him.

DOUG Or yourself.

CHARLIE Him.

WINNIE He's alright.

CHARLIE I love him.

DOUG Or yourself.

CHARLIE Him. I bring the world to him.

WINNIE Your world.

DOUG Not our world.

CHARLIE A peck of dirt –

DOUG	Before he dies?
WINNIE	He's alright.
CHARLIE	But me ...
WINNIE	She was always fond of him.
CHARLIE	I'm not alright.
DOUG	Bright.
WINNIE	We always said so.
CHARLIE	I'm not alright.
TOM	Poor Charlie. Poor Tom. Poor. Piteous.
CHARLIE	Listen. You have to listen.
DOUG	I choose not to hear that.
WINNIE	I choose not to.
CHARLIE	(a cry) Tom.
TOM	(a shout) Charlie.
	(WINNIE and DOUG exit.)

SCENE TEN

CHARLIE is looking down on TOM who is on his bean bag.

CHARLIE	Right, Tom. Time for an update. Update time. Star date ... Where did we get to? I told you about the river ... and the bridges ... now, let's see. People. Where will I start ? Well, there's Sheila. She's, oh, I dunno, about thirty five, forty ... old anyway. She wears black overalls from Milletts and she drinks real ale and cries into it because none of the men fancy her! Then she gets pissed and she sits in the corner glaring at the men and muttering 'castrate the bastards!' and 'Ireland for the Irish' and all that sort of stuff. Anyway, she's sex mad. Permanently randy. Bernadette says she had

a transplant and they made a terrible mistake
and gave her fully functioning monkey
glands. You'd like Bernadette. She's only
there at weekends. She's a Catholic. She
works in a steakhouse and she's in love with
this horrible old married man. Manager of a
cut price supermarket. Really gross. To add
insult to injury she turned vegan last week.
Can you believe it, Tom ? A sinning Catholic
vegan serving up bloody steaks all day long.
My God, it's pure Edna O'Brien! And the
town! Oh, God, I wish I could show you the
town, Tommy. I walk around it, saying to
myself, "You're here, Charlie. Here. Look.
Look and remember." I don't want to forget
any of it, not one bit of it! And the gigs! Oh,
no, I was telling you about the town. Remind
me about the bands, eh? This is me, going
out to a lecture. Slam the door, scramble past
the bikes in the passage, bloody things. Down
the steps, one, two, three. There! And the
street's so narrow – a back street in any other
town, and God! There's loads of us, some in
a rush, some strolling, great gangs all talking
together, no one looking where they're going,
like some big noisy crab, sideways. Some
riding bikes. Millions riding bikes! Here
comes one now – looking back over his
shoulder calling to someone – he hasn't seen
me, damn man! (*She flattens herself against an
imaginary wall and flops down with relief at his
passing.*) Phew! He's gone! (*She laughs and
caresses* TOM's *face, then grows suddenly quiet,
reflective.*) And it's all so lonely. I sit in my
room and I think of you, Tom. I think of you
and wonder about you. It's nothing like I'd
imagined. And I can't tell Dad, can I? You're
doing it for all of us, Charlotte, consolation
for how things are. Consolation prize. Oh,
Tom. Twenty four years old and stuck here
with Mum and Dad. You're looking at me,

Tom and I haven't a bloody clue what you're
making of all this. If you're making anything
of it at all. Are you with me, Tom? Are you?
Talcumed and combed and laid to rest on a
clean and comfy bean bag ... (*He laughs
apparently involuntarily as a baby laughs with
wind, and this suddenly angers her*.) Do you give
a damn what happens to me? Do you?
Wasting my time. Wasting my time, because
you don't care, do you? You don't give a
damn if I'm here or there or dead or bloody
gone, do you? I'm sorry, Tom. I'm sorry. You
do care, don't you ? You do listen. It's our
bargain, isn't it? If I talk, you'll listen. It's
them that make me like this. Them with all
their 'Off the bed, Charlotte!' and 'You
know we don't like you doing that', so prissy
and shut-off and we-can-cope-ish. And they
want to shut you off, too. As if you're some
timid little baby needing total protection in a
sealed bloody unit. Well, you're not. You're a
man. A fully grown, fully blown man. Look
at your beard, Tom. Feel it! (*She puts his hand
to his chin.*) If it wasn't for some senseless
accident of, God knows what, a long labour,
sloppy nurses at a slow delivery – God knows,
you'd be down at the pub right now, out
there with the rest of them – fornicating with
the best of them. And you're in working
order, Tom, I know that, too. See, there are
no secrets between us. Remember how I
helped Mum to get you up, sometimes? (*She
nuzzles into* TOM'S *neck and puts her arm around
him. After a short time* CHARLIE *draws back from*
TOM, *looking down at him, loving him. She slowly
takes off her shirt, watching him all the time. His
head jerks away and she slowly, gently, moves into
his eye line again.*)

STEPHEN   When you walk up the path you're struck by
the order of it all. Regimental. I can just see
her now, slaughtering each weed as it pokes

its little head above the ground. Him,
relentlessly advancing on the ranks of grass
with his grinding ravenous mower. "We like
to keep busy". A small and shining house. A
credit to them all. Enough to make you weep.

(STEPHEN *draws nearer to the area where* TOM
and CHARLIE *lie.* CHARLIE *is astride* TOM *now,
bare breasted, trying to make him look at her.
Wherever she moves he twists away, In the start of
a fit. She doesn't recognise the fit, so involved with
her own emotions. She takes his stiff, splayed hand
and places it on her breast.* TOM *convulses, she
scrambles off him, automatically moves something
out of his way, and then she sits, watching.* TOM *is
groaning now as he thrashes around. She starts to
cry and pulls her shirt on, all the time watching*
TOM. *Soon she is openly weeping. After a moment
she goes to* TOM *and wipes his mouth.* STEPHEN
appears behind her.)

STEPHEN   Erm.

(*Charlie spins around and almost slips.*)

STEPHEN   I'm sorry.

CHARLIE   (*afraid*) What do you want?

STEPHEN   Stephen. Tom's social worker. I'm sorry, I
rang twice. Then, when I saw the back door
standing open like that, I wondered if
anything was wrong.

CHARLIE   Wrong? Why should anything be wrong?

STEPHEN   Look. Can we start again? I'm Steve. Tom's
social worker. Well, the family's. And you
must be Charlotte.

CHARLIE   I must be, mustn't I?

STEPHEN   Are you alright?

CHARLIE   I've been having a bit of a weep, actually. Put
it down to hormones.

STEPHEN   We all need a weep from time to time.

CHARLIE	Do we? (*Relenting.*) You've missed Mum and Dad. They've gone out shopping. As soon as I walk in one door they grab their bags and run out of the other. Only chance they get to go together. Have a walk around and a cup of coffee like any other couple.
STEPHEN	Yes. (*He goes to crouch down by* TOM.) Hello, Tom. It's Stephen.
	(TOM *snores gently.*)
STEPHEN	(*louder*) It's Stephen, here to help you. (*To* CHARLIE.) How is he?
CHARLIE	I don't know.
STEPHEN	Hello, Tom. Hello.
CHARLIE	They shouldn't be long.
STEPHEN	(*still looking at* TOM) Right.
CHARLIE	Sit down.
STEPHEN	(*not doing so*) Do you see any changes in him?
CHARLIE	Changes?
STEPHEN	Going away as you do. You know.
CHARLIE	Should I? He's a bit thinner. More frail. (*Pause.* STEPHEN *is still gazing at* TOM.) I wish you'd sit down.
STEPHEN	I'm very glad to have this chance to talk to you, actually. Do you mind if we talk ? About the family?
CHARLIE	If we must.
STEPHEN	It's just that I don't seem to be getting anywhere with your parents.
CHARLIE	No?
STEPHEN	And they seem edgy.
CHARLIE	Do they?

STEPHEN	More worried, tense ... even than they usually are. From what I've seen of them, that is.
CHARLIE	(*bored*) Yes.
STEPHEN	Please. Charlotte.
CHARLIE	Charlie. I'm more than Tom's sister, you know. I like to be called Charlie.
STEPHEN	I'm sorry. I didn't know.
CHARLIE	Not in your files, that bit? I do have a personality all of my own.
STEPHEN	Of course.
CHARLIE	There's no 'of course' about it.
STEPHEN	God, this is so hard.
CHARLIE	Yes. Isn't it?
STEPHEN	(*plunging in*) I'm worried about Tom.
CHARLIE	(*her animosity begins to ease*) Worried?
STEPHEN	Concerned.
CHARLIE	Go on.
STEPHEN	I don't quite know how to put it into words. Tom. He's got something special. Some power. There's something powerful about him. Compelling. As if there's a real, hard intelligence there. I really feel as if there's a real intelligence there.
CHARLIE	And? It doesn't do him much good saying that. Or anyone else.
STEPHEN	It's a start.
CHARLIE	Don't fool yourself. A start to nothing. Others have seen what you've seen. Me, for a start. Then there was the district nurse, and some sort of education official, and when he got pneumonia one year there was the whole

bloody staff of the medical ward. All charmed by Tom Davies.

There's been all sorts. (*She takes* TOM's *leg and waves a foot at* STEPHEN.) Wave a leg at him, Tom. Yoo hoo! Here we are! Go to the back of the queue. You've actually joined rather a large body of opinion.

STEPHEN   But they treat him as if . . .

CHARLIE   And how should they treat him?

STEPHEN   I don't know.

CHARLIE   What exactly do you want them to do?

STEPHEN   I just don't know but . . . Widen his experience, change their attitudes–

CHARLIE   Sounds good. Be specific. (*Looks at* TOM, *still snoring.*) Tell him to be specific, Tom.

STEPHEN   That would need discussion.

CHARLIE   'Discussion' – What, as in 'options' and 'alternatives'?

STEPHEN   They won't discuss anything.

CHARLIE   They pride themselves on managing. Standing on their own two feet. Four feet.

STEPHEN   Is it so terrible, accepting a helping hand?

CHARLIE   You don't have to convert me. I'm just the piggy in the middle, I am. Look, twenty four years ago there was no help to be had. They've got into the habit.

STEPHEN   There's help now, if they'll take it.

CHARLIE   (*over him*) Just a cup of tea in the ward sister's office and the advice to put the baby into a home.

STEPHEN   (*desperately trying to get through to her*) I'm afraid that they'll leave it too late. I saw marks on his wrist.

CHARLIE   What?

STEPHEN   Marks. On his wrist. Eight days ago.
             (CHARLIE *goes to look.*) Oh, they'll have faded
             by now.

CHARLIE   What sort of marks?

STEPHEN   I don't know! Marks where they lifted him or
             held him in the bath or – I don't know.
             Perhaps he marks easily.

CHARLIE   I should have locked the back door. You
             could have been anyone. Gave me a start.

STEPHEN   Does he mark easily? (*She turns away and
             begins to fiddle with* TOM.) Charlie? Please?

CHARLIE   No. No. He doesn't mark easily.

STEPHEN   Thank you.

CHARLIE   Don't thank me!

STEPHEN   It's just another piece in the jigsaw. I only
             want to help them. (*Standing up.*) I'll try to
             get back tonight.

CHARLIE   They think the world of him.

STEPHEN   I know that. I only want to make things
             better.

CHARLIE   No one ever does.

STEPHEN   (*bending down to* TOM) I'll be back, Tom. I
             will. Look at me, Tom. (*He takes* TOM's *head
             gently in his hands.*) Look at me.

CHARLIE   Leave him alone!

STEPHEN   I only –

CHARLIE   Don't move his head like that. Your will
             ruling his. Don't do it.

STEPHEN   I'm sorry.

CHARLIE   Everyone making him look at things.
             Manhandling him.

STEPHEN	Charlie . . .
CHARLIE	Mauling him. Just because you have the power.
STEPHEN	Mauling? I was only saying goodbye.
CHARLIE	You don't say 'goodbye' like that. You don't grab my head and make me look at you. Perhaps he doesn't want to look at you! To be your flawed mirror! An image of what you could have been, an image of what he should have been! Perhaps that hurts him.
STEPHEN	(*exiting*) I'm sorry.
CHARLIE	(*fighting tears*) It hurts me.

SCENE ELEVEN

Later. DOUG *enters and he and* CHARLIE *tend to* TOM.

CHARLIE	Dad . . . Dad, Mum said something on the phone last week, about you moving.
DOUG	Moving?
CHARLIE	Said you'd looked at some of the new houses over at Lawton.
DOUG	She looked. I went along with her.
CHARLIE	They any good?
DOUG	Lovely, For gerbils.
CHARLIE	You're not going, then?
DOUG	Your Mum gets a bit fed up from time to time. She sees these lovely new show houses, and they've all got shining kitchens and brand new carpets, and there are no wheelchairs and cramped back rooms, and no commodes, and she just gets a bit . . . unsettled.
CHARLIE	Poor Mum.

DOUG	We're alright, Charlie. We don't want you worrying about us. Or about Tom. He's our responsibility.
CHARLIE	And my brother. But I wasn't worried about him.
DOUG	Your Mother mentioned the vague possibility to moving at some vague time in the distant future and you panicked. Panicked that Tom might get taken into care.
CHARLIE	No. No, I didn't. Not really.
DOUG	Not really. I don't want you worrying about your brother. I don't want you limiting your horizons because of him.
CHARLIE	But I don't Dad.
DOUG	When you have a handicapped child the whole family is handicapped... and I don't want you carrying your handicap through your whole life. Listen to me, Charlie. Tom's here. Please God, he'll always be here, well, as long as we are and as long as he lives. Leave him here. Leave him here and get on with your own life.
CHARLIE	You don't.
DOUG	I can't.
CHARLIE	Perhaps I can't either – (*As the words leave her mouth* DOUG *grabs her arm.*)
DOUG	Look at this place! Look at it! Look at it!
CHARLIE	Dad, you're hurting.
DOUG	This is where your fine feelings will get you! Right here! Do you think that I could bear to see you going down a road that ended up here? Turning into someone like me? Is this what you want for your fresh young life, is it?
CHARLIE	Dad, calm down.

DOUG   Nowhere. Nothing, Going nowhere doing nothing. I don't want that for you. A lifetime of keeping Tom nice. But this is where you'll end up, and the more interest you take in him now, the stronger a hold he'll have on you. He has the grip of a drowning man. (*Pause.*) No. Don't worry about them taking Tom away. We'll never let them do that. Don't worry about anything changing. Nothing's going to change. If they were to take him away, what would be left for us? There's only Tom for us. The Tom that is, the Tom that was, the Tom that ever will be.

CHARLIE   Oh, Daddy, what will you do?

DOUG   Do? Oh, we'll carry on for a bit. For a bit longer.

(CHARLIE *exits.* DOUG *fills a medicine funnel with bright pink medicine.*)

DOUG   Here we are, Tom. Before all that lovely tea leaves your tummy.

(*He puts the funnel to* TOM's *lips.* TOM *is in a small spasm.* DOUG *waits patiently for it to pass and then tries again. It is so thick that it wells up on* TOM's *lips.*) Bloody stuff. Come on, get it in, old man. Come on, for sweet Jesus sake ... You stupid bloody ... (*He twists the funnel so that it is forced between* TOM's *lips.* TOM *appears to take it all and, just as* DOUG *is straightening up, satisfied, he spits it all back out again in a convulsive, choking cough.*)

Shit!

(*Pink medicine everywhere.* DOUG *mops it up, disgusted. Watches* TOM *warily.* TOM *calms down.* DOUG *starts to go but then* TOM *starts to choke.*)

Oh, God.

(*He pulls* TOM *off the bean bag and rolls him into his side. Panicking, he thumps between* TOM's *shoulder blades. TOM flails wildly, the choking turning into a whoop, his face congesting.)*

Oh, God! (WINNIE *runs in and makes as if to help.)*

DOUG   I'll do it! I'll do it!

WINNIE   Just rub between his shoulders, don't thump him.

DOUG   I know! I know! Just leave me alone ... leave me.

(Gradually, as he thumps and rubs the choking dies down. TOM takes a big shuddering gulp of fresh air.)

DOUG   There. See. I could manage.

WINNIE   It's all over your sleeve. I'll get a damp cloth. (DOUG *looks at his cuff with distaste.)*

DOUG   I'll see to it. You sort him out.

(WINNIE goes to TOM and with infinite patience wipes his face. She makes little soothing noises to him.)

SCENE TWELVE

Third Discord (WINNIE'S)

DOUG *enters,* WINNIE *gets up and busies herself.*

DOUG   (*sitting down*) Come and sit down Winnie.

WINNIE   I cannot sit. You know that. I can't just sit.

DOUG   Then come and talk.

WINNIE   Talk?

CHARLIE   (*entering*) Come and talk, Mother.

WINNIE   What could I talk about?

CHARLIE   Your thoughts, Mum. Your thoughts at the kitchen sink.

WINNIE	It's a small house, dear. No room for thoughts. Just wheelchairs and lifting aids and beds.
DOUG	Come and sit.
WINNIE	I must be doing.
CHARLIE	Come and listen, then.
WINNIE	I cannot hear.
DOUG	Ah, come.
WINNIE	When I was a child I could not bear to share the Penny Arrow bar my mother used to buy for me.
DOUG	Come.
WINNIE	My thoughts are without words. They have no form.
CHARLIE	Blind foetus, curled up away from the light.
WINNIE	Yes. Yes ... Suckling puppies, blind and groping.
CHARLIE	Suckling?
WINNIE	I have no will to move away.
DOUG	Then come here.
WINNIE	At my mother's house there was always a dog, and she was always called Meg.
DOUG	Come and sit beside me and let me hide my eyes against your body.
WINNIE	Always a Meg at the fireside. Two litters a year. Always the same.
DOUG	Let me nuzzle into your flattened breasts and the deep dark parts of you.
WINNIE	And I felt sorry for all those Megs when the pups were grown, but still greedy for her milk. Sharp teeth.
CHARLIE	She has no more milk to give.

WINNIE   All those Megs and all those teeth. Her back
            would arch as she tried to step away from
            their strong and angry little jaws, her tail
            tucked between her legs, and I thought,
            'How cruel. How cruel they all are.'

DOUG   Only needing comfort.

CHARLIE   Bed warm bodies.

DOUG   Finding the tit.

CHARLIE   She has no more milk to give.

DOUG   I'll find her tit. Coax from it a blessing, a
            warm sweet blessing, take it in my mouth,
            her blessing.

WINNIE   She had a wooden box in the dark corner, by
            the range. Warm and quiet. "Shush now.
            Meg has her pups."

DOUG   A drop. A trickle.

WINNIE   All those generations of Megs. In her dark
            corner. And I thought, "How cruel they all
            are."

CHARLIE   How cruel you all are.

DOUG   How cruel you are.

WINNIE   How cruel.

            (*They exit.*)

TOM   Steeephen. Steeeee phen. Stephen-here-to-
            help-you. At the end of the day Stephen.
            When I smell of fear and shit and love,
            Stephen. What, then? What then? Nothing.
            Dark nothing. And Father man. Daddy man.
            Father. Daddy. Man. Daddy. Daddy. Father!
            Bloody fucking Father! Father fucker! Fuck!
            (*The words strangle into a yell.*)

SCENE THIRTEEN

Night. DOUG *enters.*

DOUG   (*calling to* WINNIE, *off*) It's alright. He's just
              having a shout. I'll settle him down. Won't be
              long.

              (TOM *is moaning, showing discomfort.* DOUG *lifts
              his head, settles him down again on his pillows.*)

              Better? (TOM *moans again, screws his face up,
              ready for a shout.*)

              Alright, alright, hang on. (*He adjusts* TOM'S
              head again.) TOM *is silent. After a moment* DOUG
              turns to go but as soon as his back is turned TOM
              moans again. DOUG *turns back, impatient now.*)

              Shut up! Shut up! (TOM *shouts at him, battle
              declared.*) Shut up, you bloody bastard! Shut
              . . . I know what you shout. I know. After
              twenty four years, I bloody know. (*Glaring at
              each other.* TOM *gives a bark of a shout, defiant.*
              DOUG *lifts his head from the pillow and bangs it
              back down again.*)

              Bloody . . . bloody . . . (DOUG *looks around and
              sees a bib, grabs it and rams it into* TOM'S *mouth.*
              TOM *roars all the more, his face congested, limbs
              flailing. The sight incenses* DOUG *even further and
              he digs his fingers into* TOM'S *belly. Stands back,
              crying now.* TOM *still moans and thrashes.* DOUG
              grabs his head and pushes his face right into
              TOM'S *and makes a vicious face, and an angry
              choking noise. He grabs a towel and beats the bed
              and* TOM *with it, but mostly the bed, until he is
              exhausted and* TOM *is crying. He drops the towel
              and slumps onto the bed.*) See. See what you've
              done to me. Christ. Oh, Christ. (*Takes the bib
              from* TOM'S *mouth.*) Alright, Son. All done. All
              done. There now. It's all done. (*After a few
              moments* TOM *is quiet, just an occasional sob.*)
              Round and round the garden . . . like a teddy
              bear . . . One step . . Two step . . .

(Anticipating the line, TOM *takes a sharp breath in, delighted to be part of the game.* DOUG *sees the laughter welling in* TOM *and suddenly hugs him, rocking backwards and forwards, weeping. After a moment* DOUG *is calm.* TOM *is dozing.* DOUG *sits at his side, watching.)*

SCENE FOURTEEN

Day. WINNIE *enters in with a tray with a coffee for* DOUG *and a feeder cup for* TOM.

WINNIE	Look at you, you're nearly asleep.
DOUG	No I'm not. I was just telling Tom about the EEC.
WINNIE	Fat lot he wants to know about that. Or me. That Stephen phoned. He's coming over.
DOUG	Fair enough.
WINNIE	Very particular that we'd both be here.
DOUG	Well, we will be. When's he coming?
WINNIE	Before lunch. Sounded very mysterious. Will you give him his milk or will I?
DOUG	You can if you like.
WINNIE	Something about – oh, I don't know, Tom's rights to something or other.
DOUG	To what?
WINNIE	County council something or other. I had the washing machine spinning in my ear.
DOUG	Bloody hell. that's all we need isn't it ? Someone telling us about Tom's rights. Where's Charlotte?
WINNIE	Out. Meeting some of her old school pals, I think.

DOUG	It would be today. Tom and me shattered. Well, I'm not taking any old nonsense from him.
WINNIE	He means no harm.
DOUG	Oh, God, I wonder what it's all about.
WINNIE	Well, it can't be anything to worry about, can it?
DOUG	No.

(WINNIE *exits.*)

SCENE FIFTEEN

STEPHEN *enters.* DOUG *greets him with a strained, polite nod.*

DOUG	All very mysterious. All this.
STEPHEN	Not really, not really mysterious. Erm . . .
DOUG	She's just coming.
STEPHEN	And Charlotte?
DOUG	Oh, no. We try to keep her uninvolved. Free.
STEPHEN	Are you alright, Mr Davies?
DOUG	Tired. I get a bit tired.
STEPHEN	Of course.
DOUG	Not over-tired, you understand. Just tired. (WINNIE *enters and sits down, expectantly.*)
WINNIE	There we are then, all present and correct.
STEPHEN	I hope I'm not holding up your lunch?
WINNIE	Not to worry.
STEPHEN	I'll try to be quick, then. The thing is, I know what sort of pressure you're both under. Well, you must be under a certain amount of strain.
DOUG	We haven't said so, have we?

STEPHEN	No. But I can see. Looking after Tom for so long. Looking after him so well.
DOUG	He's our boy.
STEPHEN	A man now. I mean, he doesn't get any easier, does he? Lighter? And you don't get any younger either.

(They don't give him any help, only regard him steadily.)

Anyway, first thing this morning I went to the County Offices on his behalf–

DOUG	His behalf?
STEPHEN	Looking at the possibilities. What's available. To help you. How we could ease the problem of -
DOUG	Problem? Who's talking about problems?
STEPHEN	Your life – Tom's life –
DOUG	Tom's life? What do you know about Tom's life?
STEPHEN	It's my job to know about Tom's life. To know something about it. And yours. To assist you -
DOUG	We don't want any 'assistance'.
WINNIE	Oh, Stephen, we've never asked for help. Never.
STEPHEN	I felt that I had gone as far as I could go. Here. I mean, there's only so much help you can get in this environment and-
WINNIE	We don't want strangers traipsing in and out.
STEPHEN	No. That's what I mean. I thought that if Tom had a new environment. Freeing you – *(He holds out a form which DOUG disregards but WINNIE looks at.)*
DOUG	Freeing? Freeing?

STEPHEN	I filled in this form, took it to the office. Got agreement in principle.
DOUG	Agreement? What form? What's he talking about Winnie?
STEPHEN	We can take Tom. We can-
DOUG	You young bastard!
STEPHEN	Mr Davies!
WINNIE	Oh, Stephen, I don't think so, dear.
DOUG	Filling in forms! At County Offices! Forms with our names on, Winnie! You had no right!
STEPHEN	Tom! Tom has rights, Mr Davies.
	(DOUG *moves towards him and* WINNIE *restrains him.*) It's Tom's welfare and his rights that are my prime concern.
DOUG	You young bastard. So, you're going to tell me about Tom's rights, are you? You with your big red diary? You're going to be his advocate, are you?
STEPHEN	Couldn't we just sit back down and talk about this?
DOUG	Are you really arrogant enough to believe that anything you say could be more eloquent than the pleading that I see in my son's eyes?
STEPHEN	Pleading?
DOUG	Eyes that I've looked into for twenty four years? Do you?
STEPHEN	(*very still*) Why is he pleading, Mr Davies?
DOUG	My god! The arrogance of the young! Eh, Winnie?
WINNIE	(*warning him, realising that* STEPHEN *is aware*) Doug . . .

DOUG	Go on, then. Make your accusations.
STEPHEN	Mr Davies?
DOUG	Just make bloody sure that you can substantiate them... just be bloody sure!
WINNIE	Doug! Stop it!
DOUG	Because, if you can't find one mark on his body, if you can't come up with the marks, the proof, I'll have you! By God, I'll have you.
WINNIE	Doug! A holiday! (*She grabs the form and shakes it at him.*) That's what he's on about. A holiday! (*There is a silence.* DOUG *begins to laugh. The others look at him. They exit.*)

SCENE SIXTEEN

CHARLIE *enters and sits on the bed, plays with* TOM'S *hands.*

CHARLIE	(*patting one of his hands against the other*) My mother said – I never should – Play with the gypsies – In the wood –
	(WINNIE *comes to the doorway.*)
	And if I did– My mother would say –
WINNIE	There you are, Charlotte. I thought I heard the front door. Wondered where you'd got to.
CHARLIE	I'm here.
WINNIE	Well, I can see that now, can't I? I hope you're not over-tiring him?
CHARLIE	Over-tiring him? What exactly is he saving his strength for, then? A marathon? The entrance exam to The Royal School Of Music? Or perhaps a one man trip around the world on a bloody ripple bed?
WINNIE	That's enough.

CHARLIE	Where's Dad?
WINNIE	Lying down. That social worker came.
CHARLIE	Dad, lying down?
WINNIE	That young man upset your Father.
CHARLIE	Why? What did he say?
WINNIE	He wants us to go on holiday.
CHARLIE	My God. No wonder Dad had the vapours.
WINNIE	It wasn't very nice. It wasn't a very nice conversation. Your Father stormed off.
CHARLIE	Well, I don't know why you don't grab at the chance. You need a holiday, Mum.
WINNIE	We need nothing.
CHARLIE	I could look after Tom.
WINNIE	Ho, yes, I'm sure.
CHARLIE	They'll send someone to help with the lifting. Mum. . . I wish you'd give it a go.
WINNIE	Anyway, it's not up to me.
CHARLIE	Of course it is. He'd listen to you.
WINNIE	What, be another voice nagging in his ear? No, thank you.
CHARLIE	What is it you're so afraid of, you two? (WINNIE *reacts to this*.) You are, aren't you? You're afraid of something.
WINNIE	Don't be so silly. I wonder if your Father did his bag?
CHARLIE	Are you afraid that someone will be able to look after Tom as well as you do? Or better? Is that it? It is, isn't it? You want to be the only ones. The holy ones. Dedicated angels. Don't you? You make me sick.

WINNIE	(*stung by this*) Why are you so angry? What have we done to deserve such anger from you?
CHARLIE	You smooth the bed. (*She grabs it from under* WINNIE'S *hands and yanks the covers so that they rumple.*)
WINNIE	Charlotte!
CHARLIE	You hang flowered wallpaper in his room. You feed him mush when the doctor told you years ago to let him *chew*.
WINNIE	We don't want him to choke. We care about him–
CHARLIE	I'm angry because you leave him in here while you watch the TV in there –
WINNIE	His epilepsy!
CHARLIE	Because all he ever gets at Christmas is a pair of socks. One year a towel. A towel! All wrapped up in Santa Claus paper. But most of all I'm angry because you never, ever kiss him! I have never seen you kiss him. Hold him. In all the years – never! Oh, not now so much, not now when he's a grown man, but then. I remember kissing him. How I used to sneak into his room and slide into bed with him, and whisper to him, silly jokes and childish stories – We grew up together but I got all the kisses and he got, what? Soapy flannels? Passive exercises?
WINNIE	He needed those things!
CHARLIE	Not only! Not only! (*Softer.*) Oh, how could you *not* kiss him? His soft, sleeping body. His long, thin limbs. The curve of his eyelashes against his bed-warmed cheeks. For Christ's sake, Mum, whatever happened to him it happened inside you. That should draw you together, shouldn't it? He looks at you as if you were a God. A shining, breathtaking God. You know he does, don't you?

WINNIE   You're so good with words, madam! (CHARLIE *flounces out.* WINNIE *smooths the bedclothes, sits down with* TOM.)

WINNIE   A litany of despair, that's what she wants. Carefully fitted into the daily timetable. She doesn't look for tears and kisses and carryings on when there are sheets to be sluiced out and the smell to be expelled in great clouds of lemon aerosol. No. She's nowhere to be seen, then, when the tears are there. Each night brings with it the dull stale promise of what is waiting, and the cruel bright echoes of what could have been. You don't miss much, do you, love? You and I eat and sleep and keep our silence and they believe themselves to be the only ones to suffer. Only them. (*Slowly kisses him.*) Time enough for that when the years are over, Tom. Time enough for that when the suffering's done. Handsome boy. Lovely child. Precious darling heart.

SCENE SEVENTEEN

Last Discord (DOUG'S)

DOUG   Everyone gets tired, don't they?

CHARLIE   No room for me here any more.

DOUG   Don't they?

WINNIE   A perfectly natural thing.

CHARLIE   So crowded.

WINNIE   Phenomena. A perfectly natural phenomena.

DOUG   I just get so bloody tired.

WINNIE   He looks him up and down, and you can see him thinking!

DOUG   He's twenty five next week.

WINNIE   Twenty five!

DOUG	Quarter of a century!
CHARLIE	All dressed up and nowhere to go.
WINNIE	A round cake this year.
CHARLIE	A slice for Tom.
WINNIE	A small slice.
DOUG	A long time.
CHARLIE	On your back.
WINNIE	Ten candles, I'd thought. Round figure.
DOUG	Twenty five to go. Piece of cake.
WINNIE	And butter icing. Pink and blue mixed. No writing, I'd thought.
DOUG	Like a nursery rhyme. Over and over.
CHARLIE	Happy birthday Tom.
DOUG	To the power of twenty five. (*Anguish.*) Twenty five years old!
CHARLIE	Like a red brick university.
DOUG	Pushing the razor up –
WINNIE	That bit there–
DOUG	I know.
TOM	Tom!
CHARLIE	My world.
WINNIE	Goodness, he can't see everything.
DOUG	My father died at seventy five.
CHARLIE	A peck of dirt.
WINNIE	We like to keep him nice.
CHARLIE	Neat and tidy.
WINNIE	Safe and sound.
DOUG	Snug as a bug.

CHARLIE	Mutt and Jeff.
DOUG	My father died at seventy five.
CHARLIE	And his father died at seventy five.
WINNIE	Down hill all the way!
DOUG	Brakes off, then!
WINNIE	He always made me laugh.
DOUG	To the sounds of Glenn Miller.
WINNIE	Oh, what times we had.
DOUG	I just get so bloody tired at the end of the day.
WINNIE	Slippery slope I say. Thin end of the very thin wedge.
TOM	Tom!
WINNIE	Hardly a good idea, Dear.
DOUG	I'll do his drink, shall I?
CHARLIE	Empty his bag.
DOUG	My job, that.
WINNIE	Comb his hair.
CHARLIE	Flannel and soap and one ...
DOUG	Two ...
WINNIE	Three ...
DOUG	Get it in, old man.
WINNIE	His blue today, or his green, what do you think, Daddy?
CHARLIE	Out there with the rest of them. Fornicating with the best of them.
WINNIE	Off the bed, Charlie.
TOM	Into bed Charlie.
WINNIE	Pass me that bib, Doug.

DOUG	Another fit.
WINNIE	A damp wipe, I think.
CHARLIE	Cotton bud.
TOM	Tom!
	(*Their actions mirror their words from now on, more and more frantic, nightmarish.*)
CHARLIE	Like a teddy bear.
DOUG	His poor head.
CHARLIE	One step. Two step.
DOUG	Tickle under there!
CHARLIE	The curve of his chin.
WINNIE	The hollow of his neck.
CHARLIE	White talcum in a pink tub.
DOUG	(*angrily moving away from her*) How cruel you are.
WINNIE	Three times a day.
CHARLIE	After meals.
TOM	Tom!
DOUG	A sister's love-
CHARLIE	Never enough.
TOM	Tom!
CHARLIE	Tom!
TOM	Charlie!
DOUG	Wipe.
WINNIE	And wash.
DOUG	Dry.
TOM	Tom!
WINNIE	Powder. Spoon. Wipe.

DOUG	And wash.
CHARLIE	And powder.
DOUG	And spoon. Spoon the years one at a time. Twenty five.
WINNIE	Fancy that. Twenty five years!
CHARLIE	Doesn't time fly when you're –
WINNIE	Enjoying yourself! (DOUG *screams. The women look at him, mildly surprised, and then walk off. As the scream dies away he grabs the wheelchair and wheels* TOM *to one side of the area.*)

SCENE EIGHTEEN

The garden. DOUG *enters with a deckchair which he sets up and sits in next to* TOM.

DOUG	She'll complain. She'll tell me why she left you there and ask me why I put you here. And I'll say 'Because he's light sensitive, dear.' And she'll huff and puff for a bit and say something about the vitamins in sunshine, and 'You could have told me, dear' and I'll say that I just have and she'll tell me not to snap. And I'll say I wasn't. And we'll have another frozen bloody pizza in frozen bloody silence. (*Quieter.*) I can't bear her petty thoughtless cruelties. Her bright and breezey tortures. Her blitheness. Her blindness. I will protect you from her. (*To himself.*) I can't bear her petty cruelties, but, by God, I will jealously guard my own.
WINNIE	(*entering*) Oh! I put him there!
DOUG	He asked me to take him in to the shade, dear.
WINNIE	I put him there to soak up some sun.

DOUG	He did, dear. Enough to take away what little sight he has.
WINNIE	The doctor said that he must have –
DOUG	His eyes burned out?
WINNIE	If you're going to be nasty then I think you'd better go for a walk.
DOUG	Not much point in going for a walk if I'm going to be nasty. If I'm going to be really nasty I might as well stay here, where I can put my soul and heart into it.
WINNIE	I'll do the lunch, then.
DOUG	I think I'll have my pizza unfrozen for a change.
WINNIE	You're in a very funny mood. (*She starts to go.*)
DOUG	I punish him! (*She stops but doesn't look at him.*) I pull his hair and twist his skin. Chinese burns, I think they call them. I pull his head back and shout in his face. right in his face. I pinch him. I take an ear in each hand and I squeeze, and I squeeze, hard. And his eyes stare and his legs thrash and I loathe him. Loathe him. (WINNIE *breaks the stem of a daffodil.*) But I never leave a mark. I don't think that I have ever left a mark. But I can't be sure. Never absolutely sure. I'm afraid that one day I'll kill him. I dig my nails into his sweet white flesh when I lift him. (WINNIE *crushes the flower.*) He'll be back, that young man, that Stephen. He said that he'll be back. He looked at me, Winnie, this morning he looked at me, and he knew. Winnie. He knew.
WINNIE	Actually I thought I'd give the pizza a rest today. Scrambled eggs. I'd thought. (*She drops the flower and makes as if to go but then stops.*) I'm not a Jesuit, Doug. A father confessor.

And I'm not a fool, either. And I won't let
you treat me like one. Not you, not
Charlotte. No one's going to do that to me.
I've learned to cope with what we've got. I
get on with it and cope. I don't whine and I
don't moan, I just cope. And I don't want to
know, Doug. Do you understand me? I don't
want to know.

DOUG   I can't stop myself.

WINNIE   It's a small house, Doug. And a stale
confession.

DOUG   And there's no one else to stop me. Oh, God.
Sometimes I think I'll leave him. Not go in to
him. But then, the thought of him, sitting
awake, waiting. Waiting in the harsh electric
light, waiting in the dark, sitting there all
night long with his poor back aching and his
poor head lolling, waiting for a father who
will not come. And so, because I love him, I
go in to him and –

WINNIE   I like to watch the ballet on TV, Doug. I like
the precision. Every step planned, every
glance weighed, considered. That's how I
think of this family. Finely choreographed,
around Tom. There are some steps that I
must take and some that I must not take.
Some things I may see and some that I must
never see. In order that the ballet may go on.
(*Pause.*) I can cope with that. I'm numbed to
that. My guilty knowledge. My guilt. I don't
want yours around my neck. It's not fair,
Doug, it's not fair to tie that around my
neck. (*She goes.*)

DOUG   All the weight and warmth and stink of it.
(DOUG *remains sitting, gazing at the garden,
toying with the crushed flower.* STEPHEN *enters
and walks up to* DOUG *and looks out at the
garden with him.*)

STEPHEN	Your garden is lovely.
DOUG	Isn't it? Everything in the garden is lovely, except this. (*Holds up the flower.*) Not quite lovely, not quite perfect. Easily crushed, so she crushed it, and went to clear up shit with cheerful precision. And now the question is, did she crush it because it was imperfect? Or is it imperfect because she crushed it? What do you think?
STEPHEN	I think we need to talk.
DOUG	'Why should the aged eagle spread its wings?' Do you know poetry?
STEPHEN	A bit.
DOUG	'A bit'! Poetry is the assurance we need that we are not the fools or the monsters we think ourselves to be. That we are a part of the human condition. 'Because I do not hope to turn Desiring this man's gift and that man's scope I no longer strive towards such things. Why should the eagle spread its wings? Why should I mourn the vanished power of the usual reign?'
	Not that I ever flew very high.
	'For what is done, not to be done again, May the judgement not be too heavy upon us.'
	T.S. Eliot.
STEPHEN	It's beautiful.
DOUG	It is, isn't it? The melody of it is a comfort. An aesthetically pleasing way of saying 'Do your worst. I'm past caring.'
	(*Pause.*)
STEPHEN	There is nothing I can do. Like you said, there is no proof. And I haven't come to pass judgement.
DOUG	No. You wouldn't. We've seen them come and go, Tom and me. Twenty odd years of

professional carers. That's what you're called
now, isn't it? 'Carers'. You care and you care
and then you care some more.

STEPHEN   Somehow we've ended up on different
sides, how did that happen?

DOUG   And then you care a bit more. Relentlessly
caring. Unremittingly caring. Caring and
caring until we're ready to cry out for mercy
and lay down our arms and shamble along
behind you, defeated.

STEPHEN   No!

DOUG   Dragging us to our knees.

STEPHEN   Christ!

DOUG   And still you care! Leave us alone! For
Christ's sake, leave us alone. Twenty five
years ago there were no social workers.
Welfare officers we had then. And district
nurses and almoners. Look at your records.
See all the names. You've worn out our
carpets with your Hush Puppies, trekking
back and forth over all the years. And now
you! There has to be some sort of victory in
life, there has to be. And they told us, your
lot did, when we were sick of the screaming
and the fits and the wet bed and the bloody
awfulness of it all, that we were doing so
well. So well! My God, they'd have done
better putting a gun in our hands –

STEPHEN   Mr Davies, this isn't doing you any good-

DOUG   But if you're tired enough, and desperate
enough, and Tom doesn't respond in any
way, in any bloody way at all, day after
sodding day, you don't just need the praise.
You don't just need it, you get to bloody
believe it. You start to believe all that shit.
And if people stop saying it, if ever they stop
saying it, for any reason, if they stop saying

it, then all those years become ... futile. And the stupid thing, the funny thing, the bloody tragedy of it all, is that it's all lies.

STEPHEN   We can help you.

DOUG   Your holiday scheme, I suppose.

STEPHEN   Among other things.

DOUG   Why stop at a holiday ?

STEPHEN   Start with a holiday –

DOUG   Why not a frontal lobotomy? Why not the total removal of all memory? Here, inject my veins with morphine ... cut his bloody throat ... why stop at a holiday?

STEPHEN   We could start with a holiday.

DOUG   Why are you so terrified at the prospect of a bit of heartbreak? Life is heartbreaking. Has always been. You can't change that. You and your lot. So bloody petrified at the very idea of a bit of unhappiness that anything is preferable ... treachery, cowardice, abandonment.

STEPHEN   It's not abandonment. It's not any of those things!

DOUG   To me. Me and Tom. (DOUG *gets up and strides away to stand by* TOM *looking down at him.*)

DOUG   How could you explain to him that he hadn't been abandoned?

STEPHEN   For one week.

DOUG   For five minutes. He cries at night. I sit with him. How could I leave him for a week?

STEPHEN   That isn't why.

DOUG   What?

STEPHEN   I know why you won't leave him. The marks you spoke of.

DOUG	There are no marks!
STEPHEN	Not now, no. But tomorrow? If we agreed to take him tomorrow? Would there be no marks then? You're afraid that there would be, aren't you?

(DOUG *is staring at him, horrified.*)

STEPHEN	You don't know what you'll do to him between now and tomorrow, now and next week. You just don't know, do you?
DOUG	(*recovering*) What game is this? Cat and mouse? Hobson's choice? Well, whatever game it is, you can stuff it!
STEPHEN	Are you hurting your son, Mr Davies? Doug, are you ill treating Tom?
DOUG	We have looked after him for so long.
STEPHEN	If we can be honest now we can make some good come of all this –
DOUG	And if not?
STEPHEN	It would be a police matter.
DOUG	Police?
STEPHEN	But without proof . . . I don't know.
DOUG	(*very calm now*) Who else have you told?
STEPHEN	Told? Well, everyone.
DOUG	Everyone?
STEPHEN	It's not a game, Mr Davies. I've told everyone of my suspicions. All they are at the moment, isn't it? Legally.
DOUG	Who? Who have you told? The Doctor? (STEPHEN *nods.*) The physio? (*Nod.*) The hospital? My God! You bastard!
STEPHEN	Will you let us help you?
DOUG	Help? How? Watching me and watching Tom, examining Tom, talking to Charlotte,

to Winnie, earnest young men with
understanding eyes? Help? With everyone
knowing? Everyone 'understanding'?
Everyone?

STEPHEN   I had no choice. What else could I do?

DOUG   Christ knows. So. Now the praise has –
            finally–stopped. The victory is . . . gone. The
            lies are seen. The bag has no cat in it. Please.
            Please. Go.

STEPHEN   May I just have a word with Tom?

DOUG   My house.

STEPHEN   Doug.

DOUG   Goodbye, Stephen.

SCENE NINETEEN

*The garden, evening. DOUG goes off and returns wheeling TOM.
He puts the chair next to the wheelchair. DOUG goes off and comes
back again with a bottle of whisky, a bottle of TOM'S pink medicine
and a glass. DOUG sips his whisky, enjoying the evening sunshine.
TOM is peaceful. [N.B. This scene is not continuous, we slip in
and out of it. As the scene goes on DOUG becomes steadily drunker
and more drugged, TOM becomes restless, anxious.]*

DOUG   So. Here we are, Tom. At the end of the day.
            Charlotte is on the train, rushing thankfully
            back to her friends, and your Mother is
            upstairs, with one of her heads, and we are
            here. So. Here we are. Father and son. But
            we're not alone, Tom. Never to be alone
            again if they have their way. From now on
            we'll know that they're there. That they
            know. Pushing back your sleeve and
            examining the flesh. Ghouls! Buggers! But
            the night's just as long as ever it was, and I'm
            still weary, and you still need to be changed,
            to be turned, to be fed, comforted. And I

can't trust myself any more. Or her. And
they can't stop me, and she won't stop me.
Your nails need cutting. And, seeing the
tension between us all, shimmering like heat
on a long hard road, they treble it. Seeking to
diminish it, they magnify it. (*Sings.*) 'My soul
doth magnify the Lord.' Mine doesn't. Mine
bloody doesn't. Does yours? No? It's a
bugger, isn't it? We should have sat like this
more often. Father and son. God it's years
since I had a skinful. Medicine to make
everything better. Every little thing.

(*Pours some into his whisky tumbler, a little
fuddled now.*)

Raw, bleeding, foul, noxious things; cured.
Sins of omission and commission; mended.
Dank hidden deeds; obliterated. Frantic,
obscene thoughts – all made well again!

(*Toasts* TOM *with the tumbler and takes a gulp.*)

Christ! No wonder you shouted.

(*He quickly sloshes some whisky into the tumbler
and swigs it back but the taste is still foul. He gets
up and finds* TOM'S *feeder cup, unscrews the top,
pours whisky into it and takes a drink.*)

That's better.

(*He places the whisky and medicine bottles
together.*)

Quite a nice way to go, don't you think? Pink
and amber. Boudoir colours. Oh, God.
Regard this, Tom, as a confessional. Will
you? Good lad. 'She has been forgiven much,
therefore she loves much.' Well, I'm the
other side of the coin. I have loved much and
therefore I need to be forgiven much. The
other side of the coin. Tails I lose. I did love
you, Tom. Christ, how I loved you. That's
not right, I do love you. Christ how I do love
you. See?

(*He takes a gulp of medicine from the bottle and washes it down with whisky straight from the bottle.*)

No. Do it properly. (*Pours the whisky into the cup.*) You are my life and my mind. You are in my waking and in my sleeping. You are in my gut and in my blood and I love you. Love you. (*Another big gulp of whisky. He retches.* TOM *is growing more and more agitated.*) It doesn't do you any good if it tastes nice. You're a good lad, Tom, you are. (DOUG *shivers.*)You cold? You cold, son? You shouldn't be out here in the cold. Here . . . (*Struggles out of the cardigan.*) Have this. (*Drapes it over* TOM *clumsily.* TOM *is crying now.*) there you are, son. Tell you a secret? Your mother's pills . . . I took them all. One and all. Clever, eh? Not just a pretty face, your old Dad. If the booze doesn't get me the happy pills will. Pills will . . . pills will . . . pig's swill. Can't bear them knowing, see. Looking and seeing. All the years come to nothing. All the things they said, over all the years, come to nothing. I wanted to be such a good father, Tom. Such a good . . . Oh, Tom, don't cry. Don't cry. There's a good lad. Nothing to cry for, Tom. Lots and lots of people, Tom. All going to look after you . . . You'll be alright, you'll see. There now, there . . . shhh. Shush. Don't cry, son, don't cry. It's all over, Tom, all over. (DOUG *appears to fall asleep.* TOM *is thrashing wildly now, he cries out.* DOUG *stirs.*) All the weight and warmth and stink of it . . . (DOUG *sleeps on to death.* TOM *shouts in anguish. He manages to knock* DOUG's *knee.* DOUG's *head slumps. Gradually* TOM *quietens, wide eyed with grief.*)

(*Slow fade.*)

PROPS LIST

Wheelchair
Bed
Chair
Table
Vase of flowers
Stool, cushion
Bean bag chair
Stencilling machine (DUPLICATOR)
Rug (TOM)
China cup and saucer (DOUG)
Biscuits (DOUG)
Talcum powder (WINNIE)
Hair brush (WINNIE)
Flannel (WINNIE)
Tom's drinking cup (WINNIE)
Tom's Bib (WINNIE)
Tray with Tom's dinner, spoon (WINNIE)
Catheter bag (TOM)
Plastic jug (DOUG)
Comb (DOUG)
Deckchair (DOUG)
Daffodils (WINNIE)
Medicine Funnel (DOUG)
Bottle of pink medicine (DOUG)
Towel (DOUG)
Coffee cup (DOUG)
Bottle of whisky (DOUG)
Glass tumbler (DOUG)